Lost in Translation:

A collection of works seeking an
understanding of human experiences

Micah Speed

I dedicate these works to my ever-supportive family. Thank you for loving me and bestowing me with creative gifts, strong morals, and a mustard seed of faith. I love you.

"You're worth more"
- Yolanda Speed

CONTENTS

INTRODUCTION

Lost in Translation is a collection of works from developmental stages of my life. The different poems each can mean multiple things to different people. The poems use decisive speech in abstract setting to create the illusion of understanding we all sometime subscribe to. Like life, time, aging, and every aspect of interaction, these pieces yearn to be comprehended fully, but can often be misleading, or otherwise indigestible. The point of this was to find comfort in discomfort, because if life, and art, never expand the bounds of our comfort zones, then both become utterly useless.

It's poetry.

Lost

A Shot went off in the air and it caught my attention.

Now, I did not care about my minute intentions.

Not about the instagram followers or twitter mentions.

I was so frozen, I forgot my addiction to hiding behind intelligent diction.

Did I mention the shot?

It was so loud that the noise of the crowd barely did anything to mask it.

The shock only lasted until the last kid said with a scream "is he dead?"

I felt death's coldness at the temple of my head.

I did not completely know the cost.

Then he bent down with a grim smile and said, "You look lost".

Silent Rain

Today I heard rainfall.
It crashed and slammed violently into everything it touched.
Today I heard rainfall.
I likely reacted to its presence a bit too much.
Today I heard rainfall.
I saw it clean houses, cars, and the pavement of their week-old muck.
Today I heard rainfall,
but no one else did.

A question, before I go.

Am I what you expected?
When you saw me, and all the possibilities.
Did I disappoint?
I saw the look in your eye,
Creating fantasies in your mind of what I could be.
You were not prepared to be surprised.
That's normal.
I surprise myself sometimes too.
I'm just as much of a person as you.
I have ups, downs, and mood swings.
Parts of me that I'm learning to love,
Parts of me that you have.
Your lies create opportunities,
Hoping to lead me into a mold that fits only you.
So, again I ask,
With truth.
Am I what you expected, Dad?

When in War

My voice is losing base.
In more urgent news,
I feel like I'm slowly losing my faith.
Drifting, freely, frozen in place,
With the frequent feeling of falling in place.
I want an escape from this steady pace of hate.
How hard is the damn rock I keep hitting?
When is it enough?
I have yet to feel the unadulterated, divine love
From heaven above that's meant to shield my scar tissue.
My number one issue,
Is the constant misuse of the gifts you gave.
I'll dig my own grave,
And lie in this god-forsaken bed that I've made,
If you remove me from this mess, unscathed.

The baptism waters said that I'm saved,
I saved that line.
My crime does not fit this punishment.
I've given my heart in crumbled bits,
And they pummeled it.
If I could stop it all, I would.
If only I could.
Maybe I should.

I sing the Blues when...

I sing the Blues when I'm far from home.
To myself most often.
I sing the blues when I'm far from serinity,
And peace surrounds me in a chaotic time.
I sing with no chorus,
And rarely do I even understand the song,
I sing the Blues only,
When somethings wrong.

I feel I feel too much

I feel rushed.
Like I haven't had time to catch my breath.
I feel inspired,
But I was too tired to start the run.
I feel like everything around me is fake,
And well-placed to set the stage for a Shakespearean heartbreak.
A play of words so full,
That even birds would fly and spread the word.
I feel fire,
Lit by a match made of disappointment,
But made steady by steady hands my patience courted.
My faith is yet to be rewarded,
And my prayers have not yet been answered.

I feel unheard.

A bag full of hope

I hope my pace makes time.
A single step out line,
And when I opened my eyes all I saw was Black.
It made think that God called me back,
He must've seen How far I was off track,
And under attack,
And over-relaxed,
And Semi-trapped in the mindset of eternity.
Thinking I had forever to accomplish what he told me.
He said something,
But I guess I missed it.
I wish the message was up for a double take.
He must've made a mistake,
He gave me no staff to split doubt's lake,
For God's sake at this rate,
I won't have time to take off life restraints.
I hope I have enough time.
I hope I am enough.

Soundproof day

It was a rough day.
Nothing happened,
It was just quiet.
Quiet enough for insecurities to sneak up.
Robbed of all senses and no way to feel God's touch.
So quiet that I had to speak louder.
Projecting my voice as my inner child cowards away.
I let the cold waters of the shower wash away my sins of the day,
But the muck is too stuck,
And too comfortable.

I wish I could hear guidance,
But I can't.
So I enjoy the silence.

In

As I walked through the darkness, I began to feel it,
This is something real.
It's unlike anything I've felt before.
Maybe once, but the feeling was inviting.
It's raw, painful, dreadful, and sore
It's,
In short,
Exciting.
I don't know if it was the feeling or the sound that caught my attention,
But nevertheless,
It was enticing.
Its ring cut through all of the tension between fact and fiction,
Did I mention the shot?
I snapped my fingers and arrived on the spot when I heard someone ask "Is he dead?"
The kid stayed still as I brushed my fingers through his head.
I gazed at him for a while,
And could've sworn we had already met.
I looked down, smiled, and said, "You look lost".
I assumed he already knew that I was Death,
But he smiled back, which never happens,
And made me cross.
He rose to his feet and towards me he crept.
He grew bigger and when he was done, my stature barely broke his shin.
He then sat down and said, "Thank you for letting me in".

Leap of Faith

One foot in front of the other,
and a Jump across the abyss.
I just can't shake the question,
What if I miss?
Summer leaves fall in autumn,
Northern winters chill my bones.
I just can't shake this feeling,
that I'm doing this all wrong.
One foot in front of the other.
It's simple, that's all it takes.
And if I fall and perish,
At least I took a leap of faith.

Eviction Notice, With Love

I have gotten used to being oblivious.
I have become a master of mimicking the world's hideous features.
I have had to squeeze even when I know there's nothing there.
I have fought knowing the outcome
And screamed with no voice.
I now hold my stare into ignorance's eyes and dig my heels deep
into the earth before I lunge.
The jump to conquer the unknown.
Dare to explore the truth;
Those places my mind won't go.
My vincibility is dependent on what I know can harm.
I sound every internal alarm and barricade my broken heart with
a broken man, heavily armed.
My fate is starred but scared from my fight with stupidity.
The vulnerability of my identity has shown itself.
I remember building you, I said to him.
I remember taking characteristics of lesser men and stuffing them
into a tight-fit brim to fit in.

I remember wanting to be you so bad that it would hurt.
I have wanted to be you for as long as I could remember And now that I am,
I'm angry at your deception.
I am angry that I see your cold eyes in my reflection,
I'm mad this nigga has blocked good blessings.
You were meant to be temporary.
Only until, I used to say.
Well,
Your lease ran out today and you are getting evicted.
Take your baggage, desires, and need for notoriety and perfection.
You're angry and passive-aggressive and I,
From here on out,
Unburden myself from it.
From you.
You will be a distant memory in my testimony.
I am not you anymore.
You are a death that few will mourn.
I used to want to hate you.
Now the resentment is replaced with appreciation
Because without you I would still be envious.
Without you, those dark places would have been lit and I would have never grown.
Without you, I would have never experienced guilt.
I used to want to hate you, but I don't.
I love you because you were me when I wasn't.

Dark Blue Reflection

Left I look,
But right is where my head turned.
I mistook the heat of the fire,
And it burned my hands off.
I finally take the mask off,
But I'm turned by what I see.

So I collapse under the pressure of the deep, blue sea.
Oh, how free it is.
Untamed by the shores that are meant to hold it.
How does it remain reluctant,
And flows with winds of uncertainty.
Beautiful, but unruly.
Truly a sight to behold.
Ice cold to the touch,
But comforting once fully emerged.
An enigma of freedom surges.
Reminds me that my own freedom has not yet been purchased.

Full send

Peace for me feels as rare as catching a snowflake in the summer's brisk.
I run towards conflict.
It's in my nature.
I fear if i sit too long in serenity,
I tempt the agents of evil,
Or the agents of boredom.
I found peace in a memory,
And infinite time could not express this mentality.
Call it an appreciation of life.
The world's sharpest knife couldn't cut the peace I now call mine.
My mind can try,
But I've mined for too long,
And it gets old worrying.
Hurrying to find gold with unadjusted eyes, no sight,
And blind folds.
I speak life over this black whole,
It spoke death back.

Devastation

What song plays when you think of me?
What tune do you hear amid your admiration?
I hear nothing.
I deserve nothing.
No symphony, symbols, or second thoughts.
Why can't I hear it?
New valleys get explored as I try to find Heaven,
And with every missed lesson,
I lose a piece of potential and bandwidth for growth.
I obsess to feel its press,
And with every new harvest,
I'm forced to ask God what's left.
Am I?
If so,
I must recant my position.
I know my limits and I'm no longer within them.
I have been broken like I never thought possible,
And this anger I hold now is not plausible.
What comes immediately after devastation,
More of it.
Any logic would support this,
And more fibs about the light at the end of the tunnel,
Continues to leave hope vacant.
I hate this.
There could be worse though.
I must take this.
If not me, who?
Devastation?

Troll Toll

Questions slowly start to brew,
They bubble over and cause an eruption so large,
Mountains move.
What latitude must I reach,

9

Before I can say that I'm done.
Done with excuses,
But truth is,
They're all I have.
This simple life has a complex tax.
I've long left tracks I know.
Am I meant to keep on?
Am I that strong?

Screams at a void

I pray I find my peace.
I pray I find a piece of my that prays for clarity.
No longer searching for earthly gratification.
I pray I'm not complacent,
Or become too comfortable in my own safe haven.
I pray I conquer passion.
I pray I find a balance between selfishness,
And compassion.
I pray these prayers daily,
I'd pray them harder if I knew these prayers would save me.

No way

I'm uninterested in everything.
Every ring on my cellphone is a reminder that I don't do enough.
Every song I sing are just words that cling to my spirit.
I hear it.
The self-doubt that whispers,
"You shouldn't even try".
I wish I was sad enough to cry.
I miss being mad.
At Least then I knew what it was.
I'm not confused anymore,

It's just that the glass cieling turned into iron.
I'm tired.

Well Rested

Sleep is overrated.
Sometimes, the best thing for a person is to be hated.
They say heaven is well-gated,
But the gates of hell are wide open and I feel them waiting.
There is no escaping
This hole that's gaping,
And retracing its steps to face me.
We meet eyes,
But I don't know you.
When did my mind become a home for two.
I am lost and cannot find thee.
All I see is anger dressed in guilt,
And it blinds me.
Hands restrained, mind insane, tears like rain,
And I'm propane.
Ready to blow at any moment.
Rage and turmoil soaking,
Claiming that there will be peace.
There has to be.
Maybe I just need sleep.

Man of Hypocracy

The Man of steel,
Has yet to be still,
But still stops movement around him.
But with 10 for a gram,
A bottle in hand,
Spits on pavement when he spots sin.

DNA strings tied together with lint.
Dry flowers thirst like Flint,
He squints to see the other side.
Screams loyalty,
But would take out his brother's eye out of pride.
He disguised his hatefulness and jealousy as grind.
Take a look at this guy.
He barely tries,
Yet feels frustrations rise when blessing don't fall from the skies.
He sees his brother win,
And his first thought is 'Why not me?'
Well,
I know why.

Last will of an imposter

Thoughts of a wondering mind,
Rarely finds security.
Purely just question that threatens its own safety.

Feb. 19, 2021

It's hard to find love absent of pain.
Like writing with no ink.
All I'm left with is deep defining marks that say I tried.
It's odd not being fueled by rage's scorch.
I can no longer keep jars of tears to drink from when parched.
It's okay to only know a little.

Free Skies

I think I want to be a bird.
The flight, the freedom.

It's all so appealing to me.
To see cars,
People,
The concepts
The smallness of it all.
The wind under my wings preventing my fall,
While the wild screams,
And I cling to the sound and answer its call.
Sunsets gracing my senses.
My sharp will severing the tension and attempts to latch to me.
I want to be free.
The free kind.
If I were a bird,
I'd never go backwards or below the treeline.
Until I find something more precious than freedom.

Howl from the night

The night calls too often for me to recognize any other voice.
The sun rises too early and leaves no choice,
But to close the blinds and roll over.
As I face the wall,
My misery begs for me to stay in bed one more day.
As I shake off the weight of comfort,
I look up to the sky to see darkness.
I guess I'll try again tommorow

The hills are alive

The symphony booms to the highest levels of Human
achievement.
Its instruments delicate, but sturdy.
No words are spoken when it plays,
But its message is everclear.

Perfection's never near,
But I here I stand,
Just to listen.
The Symbols clash and ask,
What is it you search for?
You have experienced beauty to its fullest potential,
Yet you search more.
What are you missing here?
We grant awe-inspiring sounds and experiences,
So, I ask you?
Is it nothingness you want?
I want nothing less than a creation made by my own hands.
A new band, not cramped by old songs.
You could come with.
Be apart of the new.
I've always noticed,
No matter how far I go,
What sounds I hear,
What experiences I collect.
I always return to you.

1,2,3

Simple isn't always easy.
Breathing is simple,
Unless you're under water.
Clear isn't always clean.
The steps are ordered and marked down,
But I must wade through sewage between each.
The picture is outlined,
But sometimes the colors don't match the image.
There's a lesson there somewhere.
I just pray I see it.

Brace For Weather

The raindrops fall like stray bullets in a war zone.
Yet, I am unfazed.
The wind howls in an eerie tone,
Enticing wanders to get lost in life's maze
My memory fails.
I use the song to cut trauma's gaze.
I see youth on the other side;
Determination takes over.
I take no count of dry eyes,
Misery must rule my senses no longer.
The Gemini moves over and places the weight of knowing on my
shoulders.
The toll takes all taxes,
Cash paid.
For God's sake,
I hate the rain.

Aches and pains

I yearn for the pen's glide on this atlas.
I ache for mistakes to fix.
To make a list of all my accomplishments,
And pocket them.
At least I know I'm worth shit.
I fiend for this pen to rewrite history.
My own.
Always crowded while alone,
Wishing I was home to simply sit,
Stagnant in stone.
A heart yet froze,
And warmth in the distance.
This dilemma has not been solved in all of our existence,
And no words in any language can quantify this process.

It'd be no fun if there were.

Jan 25

I think of what I know often,
And the knowledge that I may never have.
With every breath,
I grasp the absorbed energy of ancient oxygen.
A humbling thought,
That in this point in time,
No breath is truly inaugural,
And no thought is truly unique.
With each exhale,
I let go of notions of knowingness.
I've survived knowing this,
That thoughts of hatred and violence,
Turn into a noose that lifelessness dangle from.
A neck tangled up with words never spoken.

A Glorious Ending

In dead silence, I have heard you speak.
Alone I sit and repent for the times I doubted.
I used to dread heartbreak,
The aftermath of my heartache felt like level 5 earthquakes.
Now, I embrace pain.
I know that every broken piece of me will be filled,
And every demon killed by the spill of your spirit.
I'm glad the foundation under my feet fell out,
Because I landed on something solid and unmovable.
I'm overjoyed at the scars I have because you healed them
beautifully.
You are beautiful.
You have given me a safe space to be weak,

A calming aura to surround me as I weep,
And armor strong in the thick of war.
With a blade of fire and golden dressing,
I stand diligently in the darkness,
Waiting for would-be destroyers.
They never dared show their faces.
So I took up their weapons and took their places.

Death's end

Tall tales shrinks and truth rises,
Lies lay comfortable on my tongue.
With a gasp and a punch to the gut,
I lunge.
Asking how deep the fall is.
I run,
Not asking the mileage.
Why should I concern myself with the unchangeable,
The unavoidable,
The inevitable.

Translation

After the large man spoke the scenery changed to grass, trees, and
sunlight.
Death, the man in black, refused to believe his own eyes.
Death itself had just witnessed how he took his own life.
It all started to make sense to him.
The large man smiled when he saw Death's face.
They shared an understanding.
There was no need for words because there was no mistake.
It was time for death,
Yes, Death,
To be his own fate.

A transition is hard to translate because for a while it was lost.
After the large man took death to his grave,
He realized something that made him smile.
If death is dead
What's next?
Just a mixture of noise with no discernible message.
Death is NOT two-dimensional,
It's not a concept,
And it's not the end.
The truth of death won't reveal itself to the wise or sage.
The truth is that death is simply a turn of a page.

ABOUT THE AUTHOR

Micah Speed

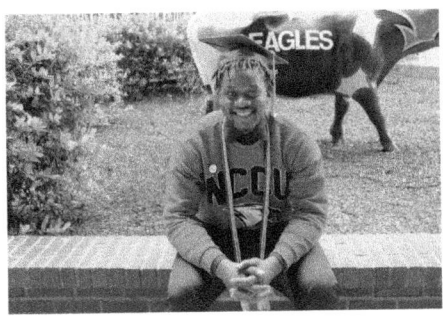

I spent time in Minneapolis and Chicago, before moving to Wake Forest, North Carolina. I graduated from Wake Forest High School and entered undergrad in 2019.

Writing and creating has always been important to me. I have been writing poetry for 8 years and have participated in many spoken words and poetry events.

I fell in love with storytelling through poetry. It was too long after when I began Crafting short stories and skits. The First short story I wrote to completion was in the spring of 2020, during a creative writing course, called "My name is Daniel".

I became interested in audio story telling in the fall of 2021, which led me to starting a podcast called Chill & Speak centered around relaxing conversations that engage the listeners intellectually.